Bohemian Rebel Naked and Exposed:
Vol. 1

by

Antron-Reshaud Brown

Poems

Bohemian Rebel Naked and Exposed vol.1

Copyright Year: 2007

ISBN: 978-0-6151-4660-7

Copyright Notice: by Antron-Reshaud Brown. All rights reserved.

Results in this copyright notice:

© 2007 by Antron-Reshaud Brown. All rights reserved.

Cover Design by
 Antron-Reshaud Brown

Publisher's Note:

This publication is to not be reproduced, stored in or introduced into a retrieval system, or transmitted, in any shape or form or by any means(electronic, mechanical, photocopying, recording or otherwise), without the prior written permission of both the copyright owner and the above publisher of this book.

This book is dedicated to
Lawrence ''L'' Warren.
Thank you for everything.

Photography by Ijumo Hayward of
Digital Phoenix Photography

Atlanta, Georgia

"When the book comes out it may hurt you -- but in order for me to do it, it had to hurt me first. I can only tell you about yourself as much as I can face about myself."

- James Baldwin

Table of Contents

Africa, Atlanta street diary entry, These dreams, Will I go?, A Blessing From Stars, I am a king, My black man, To Tyrone, Sex, Back fired...Lover desired...A Heart For Hire, Numb pt.1 Love Poem West Indian hornet's nest, Drunk, Zebra, Feminine, Just writing because, History inside of rain drops, Let's Go, The field stained red, Numb pt.2 Searching for a blessing, Letters to your secret, Descendants, Sammie, Growth, These black eyes have cried, Blade marked 666/Voice, Lust, Walking Out of The Door, His Eyes Tell it All, Fallen in love, Kicked out, Human, Circus, Hello me, Angry inheritance, Mon Cheri pt.1, Citadel, A baby cries for his mother, What kind of beautiful am I?, Overwhelmed, A kiss from white sand, His Name was Pedro, I loved you when I thought I couldn't, Red Ribbon, Off to war, Mon Cheri pt2, Gemini's many moons, Nonchalant, Five Points melody, Stood-up, Torn, Untitled Scenario, Laying here next to me, Love...Not!! Transition, Insecurity, Momma, Wearing My Pride, Innocence, I may not, Remembering, Another day goes by, Irresponsible christianity pt1, New York Brick's and A Small Town's stone, On her way to work with me, What Will Happen Tomorrow? Fire, I Need You, Bohemian Rebel, Fire starter, Black Men, Irresponsible Christianity pt2, Forgiveness, Blessed, Imagining, Without, Everyday I think about someday, Spiritual Interlude, The Best Lovin' ever, Satan's breath, Your Stories, Dance floor, The Gentleman on the Other Side of the Bridge, In your house, Jim crow 2007, Acknowledgement

Bohemian: (noun)- somebody, often a writer or artist, who doesn't live according to the conventions of society

Africa

African drums vibrating and the
Women dressed in their
Garments that are
Beautifully layered

While expressing pride
Through song and
Dance our
History
Was imprinted,
And it left
A trail of tears from
Apartheid. As dark as
Midnight, the muscular men
Hunt as a necessity.

When you look into their
Eyes of ebony, do you wonder
About the cry of Zulu warriors?
I am apart of Africa and Africa is apart of me

Atlanta street diary entry

Atlanta.
Can you get anymore beautiful?
Can your philosophy of urban living,
The soul of the South, the gay haven
Ever be diminished?
Can the streets cluttered with vehicles
Just all of a sudden disperse out of nowhere?

I think not.

Will your heart of cultural advancement
die or just simple stop beating?
Will our children stop reading?

I believe not.

Live forever,
Keep growing
Continue to rein.

These dreams
Chasing these dreams barefooted and
extending my hands to grasp them.
Some how everything seems to grow farther
apart from you.
How can we be denied of our
 Birthright to dream?
To run after dreams that lurk
in the darkness of our minds
How can you allow yourself to tell me
that I'm wrong for having ambitions
and goals?
How can you tell me not to give it nourishment
or nurture it like an unborn child?
How can you try to beat it out of me? Leaving residue
and scars of your mistakes and fears.
These dreams are my own
How is it that you can sit on your pedestal and tell me
that dreams are nothing but empty promises spoken by
a belligerent tongue.
How can you try to take it away from me.
These dreams are mine for the keeping.
You cannot steal them, nor can you stop me from
climbing that mountain top.
These dreams are mine for the keeping.
One day they will resurrect and become king.
These dreams are mine and mine alone
These dreams are my own.

Will I go

Will I go to the place where it eternally burns?
I don't understand the feelings that I feel

Why was I given these feelings?

Why is this so hard for me?

I am told constantly tales
That my father of my sky
Doesn't like the way I am.

But he loves *all* of his
Children.

I am scared.
Torn into two.

My vision needs
Correcting so they
say.

A Blessing From Stars

Writing stars on our sky.
Collecting earth and feeling
the wind between my toes.
The grass tickles, relaxed
in your arms, built from muscle.
Writing an entry in my alleged
journal, I fold my message and kiss
it to bring it good luck. You
accept and kiss me, as a way of
saying thank you. Your lips are
interpreting the stars language.
And I am smitten by your
boyishly crooked smile. The moon
laughs of joy while the universe
tells the good news to one another.
We are in love! We are in love.

I am a King

I can't believe you thought your blasphemy
Was going to work on me. Getting in my pants...
Brotha please!! You can't get it for free.
They say this is a free country but in my world
You have no access. Never will you taste my nectar
Or take a sniff of my finesse.
I am a king indeed... indeed I am a king.
I am a Nubian prince appointed to greatness by God
Never will I dishonor nor denounce my throne just so you
Can "Bone".
I am a King indeed...indeed <u>I am a King.</u>

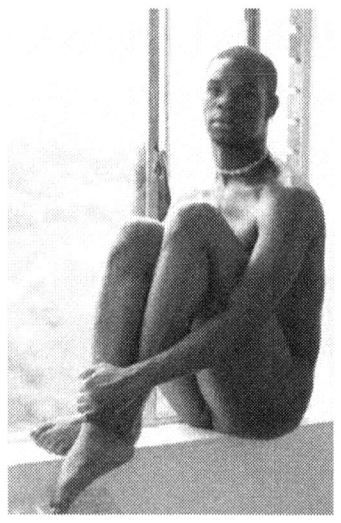

My black man

My man, my black man.
The only one that understands
Struggle and strife. The one that
Can make love to his lovers and wife.
My man, my black man
For he is king where corner stores and
Ghettos reign. It's such a simple thing
To fall in love with him,
For he is all.
My man, my black man
He will always have my heart.
From the bitter end to the fresh
Start. He and I will never part for he is..
My man, my black man.

To Tyrone

I want the caramel from your body
to drip onto my ebony. Feeling me
up and gazing. Tall and a body
like a god. He's grabbing my
submissive shape
and giving it the highest of praise.
But getting to know my mind is what
leads to *this*. We can't do *this* until
we do *that* first. You are the fiery
red that is missing in my collection
of colors. The stars can't be lit
without you. Become my Prince Charming
and slay these troubles away.

Sex

The heavy breathing is a language resurrecting when I feel
You erecting inside. I look into his eyes as my
"Lovely" is presented pleasure in between
My scrumptious thighs.

I feel a piece of his spirit conjoining with mine
And loudly I scream of pleasure due to his
"Intelligent Design".

The scratches on his back
Confirms his performance.

My body on his body, dripping perspiration.
 His strokes were pure and true blue and full of inspiration.
 I think of more freaky positions for us to do.

Yes. Oh Yes! Is what I bellow when
I feel the remaining of his high yellow artifact.
He knows what he's doing and he does it well...
My soul burns and dwells and gives into
the authority of his sexing.

Bed post breaking slowly, I looked in his eyes
and asked him to hold me.
 To Console and comfort me, while coming.
He holds me tightly.
Pampering my needs
and taking heed
 that in his mind,
this feeding of my exotic needing
is only for one night.

Back fired...lover desired...a heart for hire.

So much is on my mind
Wish I could turn the hands of time.
But not like a bitter valentine, this heart
Of mine speaks of the truth and divine.

Why is it such a crime? If I've lied would
I be able to sit back and recline while someone
Else's world crumbles and tumbles in front of my face?

His true lies are revealed but the veil
Is placed back on by denial.
It would be a while before I give myself to another.
The guy he cheated on wasn't even a brother.
His lover was pale and blinded by Cupid.
How could he be so damn stupid?
He's helping his cheating lover to cover up the truth.
I guess it was his way to cope and sooth.

He took me and I willingly let him rape me of my integrity
without knowledge that he too was a liar. Just like the rest
who sniffed and smelled my finesse.

Skinned my of my dignity...used me as an entity of lies and deceit.
The timing was bleak and his mind was weak.
He was tired of high class who had no ass
so he came to the streets.

Suffice to say he founded a so called low life
to play his make believe wife.
He opened the doors to my eternal core and
secretly deemed me his whore.

Didn't have a clue of what was in store. He truly
showed me how I felt before. Like a nigga on the
fields and beaten by a massa. The entire situation
became a proclaimed disaster.

You and I share the same *colour*
But here I am in your mind...deemed as your **whore.**

Rebel(noun): somebody who refuses to conform to the codes and conventions of society

Numb pt.1

I lay on my back once more to play the role of yet another man's desire. Feeling numb, inside I cry out to Jesus. But I like the attention the lust gives me. Mistaking sex for intimacy...really that's all I know. Tears flowing onto my cheeks for these thieves are stealing my royalty. I was never made to be loved, just used.

west indian hornet's nest
Swarming like killer bee's.
 Attacking my sweetness.
Hardcore they portray to be.

These men have built a nest where anyone
 of difference cannot commune in their minds.

Women are targets of objective sexuality
While I am a target of generated hatred passed down.

It is written in their stones that in their worldly nest,
The weak are not allowed and the humble aren't tolerated.

 Images is everything and if you go against it, BEWARE!
As their razor shape tongues and flying fist are ready to
Dispatch while equipped with machetes to take out the *"evil"* spirit.

Enter the West Indian Hornet's Nest at your own risk.

Prepare to be ridiculed and eaten alive.

Banty boys are non - existent.

Their rules written in blood have and will always remain
Stained in their heads.

 Echoing to *"destroy"*

Love Poem

Why must I feel as if I am betrayed?
Love has two sides and two faces
to it's every story. I have written
poetry for him and I am once again,
rejected.

Dear Love, I write to you to
tell you to go to h*ll. Because you
are full of lies. Hearts are broken
everyday. Minds are messed with everyday.
People are counting on you to make there
lives whole. But you don't come to the
rescue. It's a gimmick. The one that reels
you in dry. Like a summer's heat. Risking
everything, everyone. Just to hold in our
hands a piece of joy.

Drunk (For Cornell R)
Today I solved my problem with a bottle.
Laying down and realizing that even the nice guys
are **anal**.

Last night, he took me and wrote
his name all inside of my world.

Now, I sit here. Drunk!

Never did he stop to think about me before
he got some of me.

Truly he was a wolf in disguise.
Screwed me.
Fed me.
Fantasized with me.
And then forgot about me.
And diligently he was
proud of hurting me.

Now I sit with a bottle
Of my new lover but even it
Ran out on me.

Tired of being disappointed
Tired of being stomped on
Tired of being used as if I'm the village whore
Just tired of wondering whose in store
Just tired of crying every damn time his
rhyme turns sour.

Damn... I did it again. I was fooled once more.

Zebra

Mixing colors are delightful
Rejection is what my heart
can't handle, when it is my own
color that does it. I love Black
Men, you already know.
I am looked over, for
they prefer pale faces.
It gives me a strike of rage,
not because of their color,
but because Black Men tell me that
I am not good enough because
I am not the shade of buttermilk.
Looked over, makes scream to my
hearts content. I can sit here and
call every white man that takes away
my beautiful black man
a blue-eyed Devil. But that isn't
my caliber. It's is not their fault.
But I know that my brown skin is beautiful.

Feminine (For Cornell R)

So I'm not good enough to love
But I was good enough to screw
Sanctified church boy you are
But by far are you straight.
I'm too feminine for you to determine
Weather or not I can be with you
In the public and its streets
Holding my hand, whispering in my ear
So delicate and sweet.
The time we spent was picture perfect
How could I believe your mirage?
I bet it was fun to deceive a feminine boy
Such as me, another one to add to your collage.

Just writing because...

Just writing because there's hope
left after all.

Words bleed onto paper and today
in my mind, I will understand.

Children will grow

Men become strong
Women become stronger

I will have the last laugh.

One day we all have to
go home, but today, in my mind
I will see tomorrow.

History Inside of Rain Drops

Moments like these
make me feel
Vulnerable.

Eccentric claps of
Thunder roaring
Passionately

It's no wonder why
God's so good.

He turned mere rain drops
into recordings
And notes of history.

History that is apart of us all
History that resides inside of me

At night, I hear voices
telling me to hold on
Just a little longer.

They told me about my
ancestry, inside of those
Slave ships, gasping for air
and crying out
For a dream to come true.

And how the men
and women of my beloved
Worked in those heinous
fields of cotton,
Sweating for and hoping
for a miracle to be born

So you see, God is good.
For the rain continues to pour.
And <u>we</u> are still here.

Let's Go

Let's run away together. Do you
think we'll be free?
Five dollars in my pocket, folded
into threes. Living in this life
not exactly easy. Tried of the looks
and stares. Let's go I want to go far
away from here. Let's go.. Let's be
together my dear. I don't understand
why it's so wrong. Why can't we belong.
Let's go.

The field stained red

Every blow, every kick
I knew what hatred felt like
Singing echoes but no one's
Listening.

The unraveling of my clothes left me
feeling empty, just like their
Consciences.

Hallow and filled
with shadows, revealing secrets.
And I am the mirror of those
same secrets that was in need to
be busted.

I knew what hatred felt like when
it was going inside of me
ALL OF IT.

Green grass, turning to
Corrupted red.

Two figures, standing over
My weakened and beaten
Body waiting to steal a piece
Of me.

Our futures
Dripping onto my body

Tears have dried
The worst was over

Left to die, thirsty
For assistance hungry
For security
And I have yet never told
A soul.

Numb pt.2

With teary eyes I watch attractive men, grinning as I emotionally take their unemotional strokes. I have once again, given myself up willingly. Sometimes, there's a battle going on in my mind. I try to grasp it with a simple rhyme. So I pretend to be numb as I let him willingly abuse my chances of growing integrity.

Screaming HELP ME...from me.

Searching for a blessing

I feel caged.....
Enraged and imprisoned in the hole
Deemed hell's domain. Being
Born was a crime unintentionally
Committed.

Looking outward from glass walls,
agony sings, shouts and hollers.

Imprinting this memory slowly
Bewildered I became. Trying to
Understand the pain.

Trying to see things clearer from a
Dirty window and I begin to wonder
Where is the blessing in all of this…

Calamity!

Being free is nothing more
Than a mere dream.

In shackles,

 I am bounded to the
Surface, while blown reality
Onto my face from a burning
Cigar.

Envious of the free, whose
Seem foreign to me. And
Here I am, once again, waiting
For my blessing.
Waiting while knowing that
This is when the game of life
Begins
Again and again I search for
What isn't there, but blessing will
Surely fall...after all.

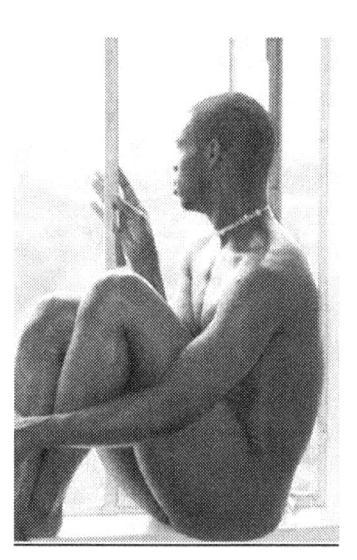

Letters to your secret

A life lead privately
Was the expression
Left when his index finger
Pressed gently against
His lips.

Enjoying it.
Indulging it.

In his eyes of ebony
I saw the word *GUILTY*
Written inside the
Tears he held within.

In his arms I felt his
Worries of being discovered.

Sworn to secrecy, I never repeated
Anything that I had to keep quiet

Descendants (to grandpa Kiner)
Belly-filled from his tales.

Smoking cigars.

 Trying hard
To understand his English.

Hat tilted to the side,
Just the way he like it.

No longer
Independent.

Guilt is what he feels
When he looks at my mother

He remembering the time he was
Once invisible to her.

Next to her are the two products
Of a broken heart.

 I look like
My mother the most.

Written on our facial features
Is the word descendant.

His mistakes written inside the wall
Of my mother's mind. Tallied onto
Paper that can never be erased.

He is trying to make up
For 39 years of abstinence.

But at the end, he will know
That we are the descendants of him.

Sammie

Where does your mind wonder when the
Addiction grows stronger?
The street corner is you house
Your job is whatever falls on your lap
You are in love with your "<u>white queen</u>"
And the town declares you as the ass.
I have sympathy for you, my hat
Is tilted for your pity.

Growth

It bleed to grow, aching are
My eternal adolescent organs
Evolving into adult parts
This skin of mine doesn't feel as soft
As usual. Another disappointed caused
My spirit to stay put. Caged once more,
Locked up by logic.
No matter how hard I try to escape
Life will always be the game and
Reality will always be the winner

These Black Eyes Have Cried

The beating and screams
It all started when I was just
Little thing.
Growing up
My sassy walk and unusual
Talk was indeed the talk of
The town, from lips and tongues
That didn't understand.
From broomsticks to telephones
To wires. I knew my place
When to talk and when to stay
In my space.
These Black Eyes Have Cried
Days were slow, carrying scars from
The nights before, while labeled a whore
When I knew nothing about sexual tendencies
Or how to loose my dear virginity
Beaten by society,
Lynched and crucified
For being on the other side.
These Black Eyes have Cried
Coming home, locked shut in my room
Her hands were heavy and the belt was
Long and stripes of gray, kicking me down
For being gay and after the beatings I can still
Till this day feel the spit on my face
When my mother looked me in the eyes and
Called me a disgrace.
  People shouted and yelled.

Wanting me to eternally burn in their hell.
Hated because of my beautiful mind
I cover the eye that soon will shine
I've seen my own blood splattered onto walls
While lying on my stomach across the hall
I am different, this is true, but why hate me
So when I care for you? Why talk about me
When I'm not around, despite if I'm nowhere near
Nowhere in sight. Just try to see, the beautiful me
For I am human too. For these black eyes have cried
On a face of black and blue.

Blade marked 666/Voice

Alone in the house. I walk into
The kitchen and awaited approval
From time. I grabbed the sharpest
Blade that I could find. Here comes
Satan. Plaguing my mind with
Intentions to end my road to glory.
Holding a blade marked 666
I raise it in the air and declare it's
Victory. Thinking, why does it matter? This
Is the end to my story. Darkness cloaked
Me as I was about to end it all. But a Voice,
Echoes into my ear to just hold on.
Dilemma came to place, confusion slapped my face.

Holding fate in my hands, I questioned
But never did I understand why. How could I be so
Worthy of life? But again a Voice echoes for me
To put down that knife. Dripping 666 all over my chest
Satan again encourages me to end it all and forever shall
I rest. But yet a Voice ensures me of a life where I'm at
My best. Unlike the rest the anointing from perfect hands
Undresses the caressing of love and comfort. The blade marked
666 was finally laid to rest, I got dressed in my armor of truth
From Satan's fire. That day I knew for sure that he was a
Liar.

Lust

As he enters my world, I said
It would be the last time
I allow lust to speak my mind for me.
It is like poison seeping out of
My pores and burning onto
My skin.

Like the
desirable hell
That I quietly
refused.

And now I sit here
Writing yet
another entry
Of my mind
and my truth.

Walking Out of the Door
(To Father Joseph Brown)

Why did you disappear out of thin air?
Leaving me here by my damn self?

Did you not see me
 while walking out of
The door?

Amnesia plagues your mind for you
Don't even know who I am anymore.

No summers at the beach or fishing trips.
Just broken birthday promises and empty
Christmas gifts.

And no more reason
to be thankful on Thanksgiving Day.
Rolling by in your fancy car with you
Fancy new life and your fancy Asian wife
And a child you adore more than life.
I used to sit where my sister sits
Laughing and smiling because you
Used to be my refuge. But now you are
Nothing to me but a pile of dust in the Sahara.

You've stolen my childhood
heart when you walked out of
that door.

His Eyes Tell it All

Sitting where you were,
trying hard to remember
you by your scent.
Eyes wonder then stops
Right on me.

He's letting me know
that sex is a must. Holding
this hand, kissing these lips
and whispers descends loudly
that you want to live inside of it.

Fallen in Love

Ever since I was a little boy
He was there, playing the role
My father was never good at.
Right beside me.

The Protector,
Comfort.
Healer.

Interfering when necessary
Sometimes I listened
Sometimes I didn't
Sometimes I never understood him
Sometimes I wondered about him
Sometimes I just wanted it my way

To tell you the truth, I've fallen in love

He will never hurt me, he will
Never lie to me.

He's the
Perfect lover...

An intelligent design

He'll just be there when the leaves of
Autumn fall or when tides change.

Embracing me with his all, his love
Stashed inside of his purified sleeves
He is perfect, he is wonderful
He is my everything...

I'm in love with **God**.

Kicked out

Disintegrating before my eyes
A punctured heart roaming
Around these streets, wondering
"*Lord* why me?"

No longer am I apart of something
No longer do I have anything to
Call my own.

To much to write down.
I feel numb.
My head hurts from the voices.
My body is tired from carrying
My nothing in boxes
A restless mind
An injured soul.

Human

To speak without words
To move without movement
and emotion.

Wooing against a wall,trying
hard to fight away the touches of mankind.

To sit still, in a lifeless room
is softly whispered into a
thousand ears.

My eyes closes and i then, remember who we
all are....Human.

Circus

The performer is ready to sell his dignity
Society will kick him down and point
fingers as if he were not a member of
The group.
He will dance, sing, shout and act for
you to love him.
He wears a mask to hide his true face.
He'll do whatever you want him
To.

Hell is a circus.. A place where you are
Exiled for being your calling.

WELCOME TO THE CIRCUS!!

Hello me

Hello me
Standing tall while
Facing a mirror
Looking closely while
Life becomes more and more
Clearer.

I feel sexy, beautiful, voluptuous,
Wanted and available. This love
Running through my veins feels
So damn incredible
I turn me on
My body feels so warm
And a smile of sunshine
Speaks heaven and depth
Of it's divine.
Hello me, you'll
Always be mine

Mon Cheri pt.1

Come away with me my love
and let us write a language
that is only encrypted in
pictures and memory books.
Under the sheets we will play
innocently and I write poetry
for to you listen and understand.
I laugh because I am happily enjoying
your company. You laugh because
your jokes are funny. Hands massages my
feet, as my pen is leading my heart
to a paper bounded heaven where I write
what I want to say. The serene voice of
Jill Scott is filling the room
with her talent and I see you,
preparing your lips to make
contact with mine. Playful I turn
away and you grab my face. Kissing me.

Angry inheritance

Now that I'm 23,
Sitting in the darkness of my old room
I watched history repeating itself.

The screaming and bundling of ambivalence
Slows my heart down and grows into a cold
Scare that I dwell inside of.

Understanding that her words can
Hurt the ones that built walls and houses
Made of brick.

This angry inheritance is passed down to yet
Another lost generation. This path looks and feels too
Familiar.

Citadel

Fortress he is the
Citadel of my existence.

Lord, how I love thee.

Cant live without you.

Can't fight with you, my citadel.

No harm will come to me
No one will break nor take me
Away from my love for him.

He will always stand tall like the
Oaks trees and skyscrapers
Casting evil away.

The same kind that keeps me down
He is and always will be my citadel...my father.

Naked: (adjective) 1. lacking covering: without the usual covering or protection. 2. not concealed, openly displayed or expressed and often threatening or disturbing

A baby cries for his mother

A black single parent
A mother wishing the best
For her child's future.
Her child cries.
She runs to his aid
Wondering why he cries so.
He is embraced in her arms
With love and guard by her touch
His tears are all dried up and she
Has secured her future.

What kind of beautiful am I?

Those boys on posters
and displays are such
eye candy.

Makes me wonder why I wasn't
born to look like them.

What Kind Of Beautiful Am I?

With their hair waving forever and forever
are they glossing their bubble gum lips
skin like buttermilk...why did I have to be
Kissed by the sun too much?

What Kind of Beautiful am I?

Their heritage is prominent and
Obvious.

Hell I had to search
for my roots.

What Kind of Beautiful Am I?

Always in a daze.
These men out here
Love the color of their skin,
Always picking me
Last because it reminds them of the past.

What Kind Of Beautiful Am I?

Overwhelmed

It's 1 a.m. I can't sleep.
Socks are off, in my underwear
Resting this body from many midnights.
Telling myself the truth this
time. I feel as if the demons are
gone, but their essence remain.
Overwhelmed, by the time's
constant ticking. Ticking because
it tells me to get myself together.
Overwhelmed by the four letter
word that is used so loosely
from the lips that say they believe
it but don't pratice what they preach.
Ovewhelmed from being alone. In a
circle that I keep repeating. No one
to hold me. No one to tell me anything
nice or sweet. Just me. Here.
Feeling Overwhelmed, Over-powered.

A kiss from white sand

Like a quiet humming....
A soft kiss that never turns bitter
in the mist.

White sand between my toes...my heart
Reaches and extends and bellows.

Echoing out loud its hellos.

Sunset arising, now I believe that
Truly I am in paradise.

I'm laying in the sand, playing, imprinting and
pressing down. Trying to hear the mystery of
God's sound.

Embracing every blessing from creation
North, South, East and West.

Just listen to the heart beats of the sand
and forever shall you rest.

His Name was Pedro

To Pedro

A reflection in this mirror
of my world his eyes sparkle
from the truth. I touch.
He touches me. Pulls me back and
tells me how much he cares by
the movement of his lips that are
pressed gently against mine. With
passion, from behind, I feel a sense
of submissiveness and security,
because he handles me like a delicate
rose whose pedals shouldn't fall. That
kiss, was what made me speak of nothing.
His tongue did all of the talking for him
and I knew then that it wasn't going to be
the last time. Pedro was his name.

I loved you when I thought I couldn't

I loved when I thought I couldn't...
When my faith was once dead.
Thinking hard to remember while lying
vaguely in my bed. Just what it was I had
said to make you react the way you did.
I loved you when I thought I couldn't...
be the pretty boy of your dreams.
When echoes become screams
growing louder. When your love
for me vastly turned sour.
I loved you when I thought I couldn't...
pretend to be your mere fantasy.
Or dress -up in masculinity so the
public eye could only see the
exterior. I couldn't live with my soul
being put to rest and hiddenly labeled
inferior
I loved you when I thought I couldn't...
Give you my all. When my life has been
predestined and written all over walls
with blood from yesteryears across the
hall.I loved you when I thought I couldn't...
Be your one true desire. The one who
could ignite and control your untamable fire.
I loved you when I thought I couldn't...
Sooth your every appetite or quench
you every thirst. Our love went from
an admirable drive to a hateful reverse
I love you when I thought I couldn't...
Change you anxious heart, to grant you
a pardon from a bitter beginning to a
fresh start.I loved you and yet I am alone. Because
of your childish insecurity..apart we have grown.

Red Ribbon

It is like a mark that will never leave
an entity digging deep and rapid
becoming permanent.
It is apart of destiny
it is a nuisance
it is both a blessing and a curse
it is a bruise that'll never heal
it is a sore that puss but never
does it buss
It is mixed emotions that leaves but return
it is the bones that have disintegrated
it is like an arranged marriage
it is the best friend we never want around
it is our worst enemy
it is destructive and handled carelessly
it is someone's wrong doing or negative
telepathy.
It is apart of culture unfortunately
but we are fighting back finally.
It is something that we want to lack
it is the answer to so many questions
it is the practice of uncommon sense
or to others it is the raping of good
bodies. It is an unattractive prostitute who
somehow makes its rounds
it is the killing of all nations
it is the source of sexual frustration
it is an unmerciful kiss
something celebrated but
never is it missed
it is the stealing of my black people
it is the end of irresponsibility
but not the end of the world.
It is the ending of old and
the beginning of the new
it is the lesson learn
some get it, some don't
it is wisdom that we refuse
it is love that keeps dying.
but it is the knowledge, strength,
self-love, devotion, dedication
and hope that drives us to
finding yet another way out.

Off to war
(dedicated to those who lost a loved one)

It was the last time I smelled his scent
while lying down, I felt a chill pressing
against my chest from his dog tag

He leaned over me and that was the last time
I felt a kiss just as innocent. I savored the
Moment with memories of him living
forever.

I felt his tears and he touched mine.
Stroking my face, reassuring me
of his return.

I knew better.

It was the last time I ran my hand
in his hair, laying preciously on his
head. It was the last time I admired his
chocolate color sprayed onto muscles.

It was the last time he'd made love to my
mind. And to decline his departure, it was
the last time he sealed his good-bye with
another kiss. These eyes withheld building
blocks of our future. And I watched every
one of them roll down my face.

It was his last time answering his calling.
It was the last time I knew love.

Mon Cheri pt2

Flash! The camera goes off!
Creating another stained
memory. The candle lit
dinner is ready. But you first
intrigue my taste buds
with a handful of luscious grapes
picked from California. Jill is
still playing. Creating *the* mood,
She speaks the truth as I end up
being in your arms. Woo me.
And lead me to the prepared table.
Softly I talk and you sharply
listen. This night was perfect.
Or close to it.

Gemini's many moons

I like him but I don't see
a future with him. Nor
do I see myself mixing his
bloodline with my bloodline
or seeing his face all the time

when we get closer the energy is kinetic
and our symmetry is perfect
but after our session of "spilling seed"
indeed I come back to my planet earth
And wish he was someone else.

Hardly able to breathe I try to figure
out why Gemini's many moon's are
attacking my temple ruled by Taurus.

I like him but I don't love him. Am I
using him emotionally? How I did I
become this addict? I don't know
weather to see what happens or
do we say our good byes and farewells.

I haven't decided.

Damn! You know love.. Or something
like it collides with judgement and fear.
But I yearn for him when he's near.
My mind isn't so clear nor sure of what
the hell we are. Are we friend's?
Are we lover? Is he the man I want
underneath my covers? But he says
the sweetest words and displays affection...
BUT is he the one I want to love and to calm
my untamable erection?

Not so sure about our platonic direction,
correction...the tainted connection between
two people. Damn... I wish this would just
disappear. But I can't help feeling the way I
do when he's near.

Nonchalant

For Tauraus

For days I haven't hear from you.
Your clothes are still hanging
in my closet, waiting to be
picked up. You don't call
and neither do I. But I
break down and pick up the receiver.
No answer. Again I call and finally
you answer. You're acting as if you don't care.

Or maybe
you're *not* acting. Those things
didn't matter after all when you
said that they did. Sounds like to me
like I need to move on.

You have.

Five points melody

Five points...
Center of it all.
From the venders on the corners
to the girls wearing tightly fitted
clothes of summer. Making men
in their minds wonder how good it
looks and feels..Well... *some* of
them anyway.

Now, today, I watch men and
women watch their children
play. I see femme boys
protesting their gay by
voguing down the streets
for the straight boys to
Secretly watch and indulge...

While holding onto their girlfriends.

Or the homeless man begging
for my change..will it ever end?
Is it a sin when you don't give
because you can't give. I barely
can feed myself let alone your
bad habits and addiction to sorrow
and depression. Smoking up my
$2.00's worth of blood and sweat
or drinking down your hopeless
regrets.
Brotha please..get off your knees
that's not the way to get paid. Why
pay for your sex when I can freely
have my sex and still get laid.

Stood-up
(to Ron...you really missed out on something good)

I've waited and waited
by the phone for him
to call me here at home.

In my mind, I hear the
ringing and in reality
nothing but silence
singing the blues

tonight I ate by myself
I danced alone, hoping
that would all change
by him just calling my
phone.

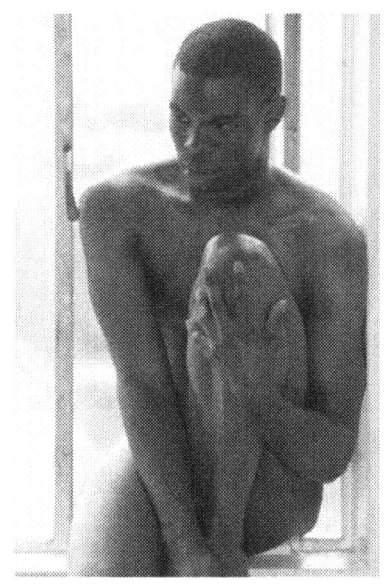

Torn

Deciphering weather it's worth it.
Wondering if everything I've worked so
hard for was worth it?

The room's so bright, surpassing
the shining lights. Blinded I am
with a dirty mind but a clean soul

Torn between me and the me I will
know one day.

Untitled Scenario

I age from knowing the truth about playing games and being tormented by a poison dipped arrow that was boomeranged by my love and hate Cupid. Honesty is out the window, when you are lying to one you love ever so.

Courage is gone when you can't admit the lie.

The truth still hurts when he doesn't return your calls. Sitting by the phone, hoping that maybe he will do what he say he will do. But you already knew that he's not going to call. Just having that hope is what makes you sit there and wait. And wait. Love is nothing but a box of tricks that we all perform, but the truth still remains stained onto your t-shirt.

Laying here next to me

I opened my eye and then realized
that the empty spot next to me
May just be a permanent marking
Where no man will ever fill.

No one will touch my face
and kiss my cheeks,
no one will watch me sleep
delicately under these sheets.

I opened my eyes and realized
that you're not next to me.
You're not here to hold me or
feed me assorted grapes and
strawberries.

I opened my eyes and then I realized
that the world has what I want and yet
you're not apart of this world, nor mine.

You're not here to compliment nor encourage
nor can you tell me just how it is that I got
so fine. "I get it from my momma" you would
incline.

 I smile from your words while laying
down next to you, listening to the language
of the birds.

I opened my eyes and realized
that someday but not today,
here is where you'll be.

Under my blanket of white
resting on my pillow of red,
in my bed laying here next to me.

Love...Not!!
(spoken word)

A lie packaged and delivered.

The boxes of chocolates are full of your
False Pretenses.
Artificial Intentions.
Truthful in corrections
Hopeful directions.

Here we are, having a
Craving for this.

Why?

GOD is real **Love**... not this
 Masculinity vs. femininity
Fucking you, me and the whole
 city being messy, yes
Being messy kind of Love.

YOU ALL ARE FOOLS... tricked to go
 To those fallacious schools
Where they teach you that "*Image is Everything*"
Hoping that man will give *You* a diamond ring.
Please, in his right mind maybe but truly he's so
Busy trying to cover up his tracks of pulling out
All of *YOUR* tracks and not his girlfriend's.

WAKE UP...LOVE DON'T LOVE NOBODY
WAKE UP....LOVE DON"T KNOW NOBODY.

Love is like crack matter of fact we all are
Addicts of the dick Love puts on us, creating
A fuss about who will win it. Love to you is
The abuse you endure to make sure you're
Never lonely again.
 Love is the number of times he has cheated.
Love is the number of times he's given his
Ass to kiss and told you to eat it.
Love is the scornfulness you feel when you

Realize he or she wasn't the real deal.

LOVE… is
the one thing that keeps us going back to the house
of rejected nobodies to find somebody.

Love is powerful.
Love is dangerous.
Love is everything
Love is nothing
Love is good
Love is painful
Love just is.

Want to be conformed,
 Reborn but scorned
And torn never was
I ever apart of the norm
By love why because
We've all gotten too high
On love and it's broken thoughts.

Transition
(to James..may you rest in peace)

I used to watch how he
would strut his stuff
on the aisle of the holy temple
and his tongue spilled
Prophecies over me like rain.

Never did I learn his folklore of life and
testimony. He is now carried by the
winds of the east. Waving forever in
oceans of the sky.

Unexplained, this transition.
You never see it coming.

But I will miss him.
The voice of pure. Like
the drumming of Zulu.

His true calling is at hand
forever will I understand.

Exposed: (transitive verb) -

1. Uncovered and therefore visible or without protection

Insecurity

Still living under ancient parental rules
carved in stone.

Envisions of boyfriends to come or
will never be.

Insecurity…that's me.

By long shot, too many times
have I derived the need for affection
or the need to release my erection

when men look at me, they see desire
inside the flames of my beautiful fire

enticing and direct, will you and shall
you burn as of yet.

Ability to connect but afraid to
approach and collect the pleasure
that I acquire...

Insecurity, that's me.

Insecurity...are we all
in a mode of self-doubt.
Gray reality cannot subdue
or agree with a colorful
point of view.
So I guess I wont fit in after all
insecurity…that is me.

Momma

you raised a revolutionary
all by yourself
making sure I gained
while you went lacking.
You've made mistakes
said the wrong things
but you raised me.
Now I am a man...a new way.
I wasn't ready for the world's bosom.
I had no choice. You pushed me
out to the wolves but I thank you
for that.
Now I understand God's plan.
He knew to plant his seed in you.
I am grown now. But never will
I forget that you tried your best.
You raised a revolutionary...
A legend.. All by yourself

Thank You.

Wearing My Pride

I hold my pride up high. Sitting inside
a coven where pale faces stare.

My color
and beauty is radiant and recognized
but unrecognized.

Their eyes scream
ancestral history.

I look no longer
into their blue eyes.

I am a descendant of Kings and Lords.
I am a Nubian and I wear it proudly.

innocence

where did you run off too?
Not knowing that I may have lost you.

I guess I grew out of your tightly fitted shirt.

No more giggles when sex enters this mind
no longer will I act out on you naively.

I just grew up today and the world taught me a lesson.

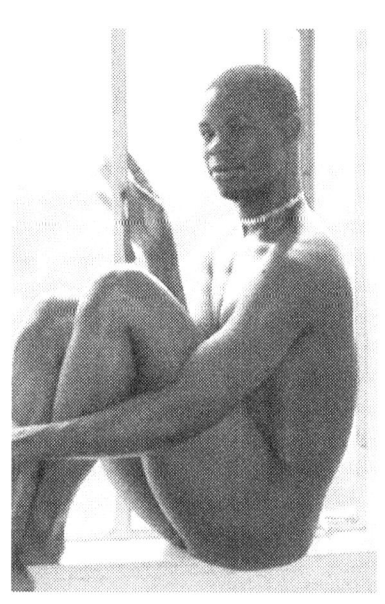

I may not

I may not be a thug with
dreaded-locks hangin' as
low as my pants.

Or a pretty boy who glances
endlessly at a mirror. Thinking
he is God's gift on earth.

I may not be a Tyson Beckford
or a Kobe. I may not be your type.
I may not be the great pretender
of the sexes.

I may not have the players card
or a swift bank account. I may not
have the biggest house or fastest car
or gold "bling-blingin" in my mouth.

But I have love, respect, worthiness
I am Antron-Reshaud...get used to it.

Remembering

My window is full of pictures
photos that constantly tell
a tall tale, photos that constantly
scream stories of the lives
that steps on the concrete

the plucking of an acoustic
guitar makes me remember
remembering memories
that are worth remembering

I remember God's Unconditional Love
I remember good times, bad times too
I remember futures and pasts, I remember my name

Another day goes by

Tonight...
Another black man was taken to jail
escorted by white hands and feet
I shake my head in disbelief.
I imagine his wife and children
crying out to him. Or maybe just maybe
no one cries for him at all.

Today ...
Another gay man was beaten
half to death by hateful hands
and feet. My soul is in grief.
I imagine his family's concern
or maybe, just maybe
no one cares if he
dies or lives,

yesterday...
Another woman was demised
and looked down upon. For she
is secretly anointed to be strong,
even stronger than most men.
I imagine her boyfriend or husband
sharing comfort in his arms. Or
maybe, just maybe
she doesn't have one at all.

Two days ago...
Another child was abused by
insecure hands and feet. I shake
my head in disbelief and you
wonder why our children run to
the streets.

Sunday...
Another fire breathing preacher
somewhere across the nation
preaches about how homosexuality
is an abomination, with a hateful
speech...I shake my head in disbelief.
I imagine the one member speaking
against the teachings. Or maybe just maybe

he doesn't have a voice nor a choice at all.

The day before yesterday...
A black man kills another black man
during a gang fight with confused hands
and feet. I shake my head with disbelief
I imagine his death making others
realize the destruction within
our people....or maybe we will
remain in ruins.

Irresponsible Christianity pt 1
(Dedicated to the black churches)

standing on that pulpit
positioning yourself as God's man.

How dare you slap my hand away from
the alter? How dare you speak of hate
in a house of love? How dare you call
my views and my standing against your
teachings blasphemous.

How can you love and hate at the same time?
Or maybe it's this rhyme I say that makes you
nervous and sweat. For your "oral" ordeal maybe
revealed. Especially after all that talk about gay
this and gay that, but yet late at night, you call
Dante over and pull out his tracks.

Preacher..preacher..trying to reach cha.. Singing
songs and hymns...but yet you have no clue.
Stop gay bashing my brothers and sisters.. For they
are your kin too.

Preacher..preacher..trying to reach cha..
You extend your hands and call out to those
who seek the Word, but you turn me away
with your words of so called "condemnation"
because I am a different form of God's creation

New York Brick's and A Small Town's stone

Venturing off to where my dreams have told me so. New York is the name that is mentioned. Momma told me not to go. Dad can't tell me anything for he's invisible. New York Brick screams stories about those who have been slammed, killed, and robbed onto them. Clashing and smashing, my tiny soul, made of a country stone is no comparison to these New York Bricks that are like a foreign country. I am that small town's stone and New York Bricks are the challenges and the way of life that is waiting for me to clash.

On her way to work with me

I have memories about the
times I was little. Wearing
baby clothes and spitting
all over my self.

Momma is taking me to the
babysitter on the bus route
I cannot recall.

Wearing a uniform that represents
her entitled agony. She knows
that she must ride this bus
to take care of me.

I remember her looking into my
big brown eyes and telling me
that she loved me. Holding
me high while I laughed with
no worries. She too laughs
and pulls the cord.

What Will Happen Tomorrow?

Will the daughters grow-up
and become good mothers?
Young boys are turning to men.

Women giving
birth to our earth. While men
suffocates from the shock
of how much their "pocketbooks"
can stretch. What will happen
tomorrow and the next day?

Fire

He touched me and I felt
the fire arising from his hands
I lean my head back and rested
on his chest.
Fire....the flames born
from passion came
from his lips as he
kisses me, meeting with
destiny.
His eyes burning heavenly
while drawing me much
closer to him and in his
arms I felt the heat.

I Need You

This world is unbearable sometimes.
I say that I can do it by myself,
but I can't. I say that I can uphold
my own. But I can't. I need you.

Whomever you are.

Bohemian Rebel

It lives inside of my bones.
Forever I am transformed
And named Bohemian.

My view is colorfully realistic
I managed to live in a world
of gray.

It circulates inside of my lungs.

I scream *Bohemia*!

 Like it is a song
that reigns forever.

I am a Bohemian.

I am a Rebel with a cause.

Inside of me is the screaming diva
Who would *let have* and protest
Till the dawn becomes night fall.

I rebel for the sake of my little brothers.
And I rebel for the safety of my little sisters
Who don't have a voice.

Fire Starter

the walls are caving inside of my eternal person.
Fire has become my butterfly, I watch it and
admire it with no desire to harm but to love.
The fire in my eyes have grown into
a force of nature. Grown into an unstoppable
flame that will burn until days are numbered

nothing will stop me.. The fire starter.

Black Men

Skin like the color of honey
reflected from the sun to the
cloak of black, I love them all.
From the corn rolls to the waves
and fades that are presented to
catch my eye. Muscular, skinny,
choices of many. I love them because
they represent the lust that I need
quenched.

Hard workers, with big hands
and other "parts". I love them because
they make me feel whole. They attract
my eye. Black Men

Irresponsible Christianity pt 2
(the answer to will I go?)

hell is not where I belong,
big momma was surely wrong
Leviticus and Romans need
not apply, because I know
I'm saved and my love
for Jesus will never die.
So those who deny my
right to the kingdom...
Look out you just called
God a lie. He's made no
mistakes on me. I am perfection in his eyes
mess with his anointed and
your world will surely collide,
collapse and relapse all over
the place..
so if you're trying to
throw Leviticus and Romans
on me, get out of my face for
I know the truth, the whole
truth and nothing but the truth
from the stories of Jonathan and
David to Naomi to Ruth.
So for you here's living proof
that I am not a defect, that my
life is surely correct.
I can't speak for everyone.
I can only speak for me.
Don't give me artificial
sympathy.
So forget what you heard
and relearn what you've
been told. As far as I'm
concerned..God and I are whole.

Forgiveness

vindictive I am not anymore

I don't wear retaliation's skin
or hate you for the bitterness
you left me and the pain you
caused.

Even thought you meant it

my heart has harden, this skin
is tougher. But I have to forgive you
anyway or I'll never see change.

Can't stop thinking about why we
didn't work. It was you who told me
to disperse. Scattered all over the floor
are letters to you like my heart was once.

I have to forgive you, no matter how hard it is
I have to speak a tongues that's acid free when
I hear your name. Letting the past go...letting us go...
Letting you go..finally I can forgive.

Blessed

watching the world
around me, growing
are these wings.
feathers earned from
years of experiences
and tribulations.
Lying quietly on the bed
wearing my naked.
cocooned and finally
my wings begin to spread.
My only way out of here.
The glass ceiling explodes
and becomes broken
pieces of crystals of my life
reflecting possibility and
potential
breaking free...
I can soar.

Imagining
(To my crush)

I wonder what his dreaded-locks
feel like when I run my hands through.

Or how his words would pour out
like a summer's dew

I want to know if his spirit and my
spirit will connect. Or if he could
whisper a song into my ears..making
love to my mind...hard and erect.

I guess it's the affect he has on me.
On my knees and on his knees.
We pray for one another.

I imagine that one day
he soon will be my lover.

Without

I push hard to make myself worthy.
Maybe destiny will be kind this time and
not walk away. <u>Without focus there is no drive
and without destiny there is no reason.</u>
One day in my life, I'll just be sailing and breezin'.

Everyday I think about someday

I want what lovers have....

I want someone's eyes to wonder
and explore.

To admire the creation of my being
and find the entrance to my core

I'm so jealous...
Excuse me for being over zealous
But I know I can love.

Everyday, moment, and hour
I think about it.

I think about how my poetry
will flow into his ears or
how I'll call his name and he
answers "yes dear'.

I think about the long walks and talks
about marriage. Or how many babies
we'll push in a carriage.

I think about our house and it's flight of
stairs. I think about growing old with him
and running hand thru his gray hair, while
rocking in our rocking chairs.

I think about how life would be if I had another
entity to share and live my dreams with. Or how
his voles of love are promising and swift.

I think about how he will make sure
that there's no "In" following "Secure"

I think about how to him, my looks could kill
no matter what happens, he will love me.

In sickness or in health, the up's and down's
and the lacking of my wealth.
Never ever will I be a trophy on the shelf

he will hold my hand with pride that's constantly
evolving and manifesting inside.

I think about how I will cook and clean or load
clothing in the washing machine.

BUT NOT HIS DRAWS....NO MA'AM!!!
I don't do those, nor will I do the windows.

That will be his ordeal for that is my Achilles heel.

I think about our sex life, the names we'll call each other
and the games we'll play and how my hunger for more of
him will make him stay and in our bed we will lay.

And in my mind to myself I'll say: "All of this will happen to
me...someday."

Spiritual Interlude

In a desert called reality
from the fountain of trouble,
under the bridges of blessings,
I will rise and like the Phoenix
of the sunset, I again will rise

The best lovin' ever

I just had the best lovin' ever

He drove right in and conquered
my endeavors.

Softly massaging the
back of my neck, all of his hairs
laying properly on his goatee

in my bed, he came and got a
taste of me.

Truly, totally and hot nasty,
his fantasies were fulfilled as
I took him over the hill
where he saw the sun rising and
the moon shining.

Whining no more "I can't anymore'

I watch and wait and relax
while we both climax and we
become satsified.

Satan's breathe

chains broken, insecurity unspoken
no more does loneliness lay in the bed of my mind at night.
Making sense of this law called precedence
no longer does self-hatred's mail comes to this residence
No longer does Satan's breathe lies into my ears whispering
"never will you suppress your fears".

Your Stories

Tell me everything and anything
that will fill this lustful
stomach with a belly full of
sexual tales that pleases my ear.

Tell the story of how you will
take my legs and enter my world
with open arms. Or the time that
you tasted my nectar and I've tasted
yours.

I want you next to me, so I feel
feminine and safe.

Hold me like you
would hold your girlfriend and take
my body and run your hands though my spots
and special places. Recite the poetry
of your tongue. It always takes me to a
different place.

Take me and I will take you.

Dance Floor
 (For the Club heads)

Leaving behind be wilderness
at the door. Stamped,
ready to get drunk
and be loud.
The room's aroma of
cigarettes and musk can
only come from one place...
The Dance Floor.
Ready to chug sorrows down
with cups and cups of my new
best friend. The DJ's playin'
my song and I feel like I belong.
Connected to the music
The constant thumping
of the speakers teaching
me its native language.
With a cup at hand
Ignoring judgment from
a cold stare, I dare
this hoe to try me, or
thrown at him will be my
chair. Without a care , I
model my new outfit as I walk
up the stairs where the boys are.
By far, as of yet, embracing the
metamorphosis taking affect. Getting
the number at the door and the lead
myself back to the Dance Floor.

The Gentleman on the Other Side of the Bridge

Wrapped in the silk that has torn
My heels are worn. From the thoughts
of wondering if I am really loved.
This gentleman has laid me down and
makes me speak in tongue.

*This gentleman
has told me that I was his for the
keeping.*

Though in my heart, I do not
believe the voices of man.

Man is a liar
that boroughs, trying to find a soul
to attract and weaken. I find myself
truly and honestly alone....

Sitting in a chair, the chill from its
steel feels the way that I do when your back turned from my

"I Love You"

No word from him.

This too shall pass.

In Your House

Sex marked on sheets
where I once laid. Greg laid
down with me. Our sweat
fountains like a christened
bottle of glamorous champagne.
But you decided to repeat history
with someone close to me. Greg laid down
with me and Timothy.

I guess I was nothing more then a tool,
No respect from the both of you.
Inside of me confession burns
Inside of me hatred rises.

Hiding painful lies behind
those innocent and angelic
eyes of his.

If I look at you, I may just melt
If I hear you, my ears will bleed.

Jim Crow 2007

I now know what it is like to have
the word NIGGER hanging
off of my neck. Glittering with
those deceiving diamonds.
It makes me disdained when it is
harder for blacks to move up.
Call me prejudice
which before I was Uncle Tom
Call me whatever you like.
Admit it Jim Crow, you have
banked off of inventions, poetry,
and other creations that manifested
from black hands.

And now,
you're making it even harder
for a black boy from the South
who possess smarts and cleverness.
We have fought for so long
But dammit I am tired of
fighting. I am tired of Jim
Crow's ignorance blocking
my damn view.
We never asked to come to
this land you call America.
We were fine in our huts, doing
our dances. I want answers
and I want them now.
Teachers ain't teachin' them.
Either they can't or won't speak
truthfully.

Jim Crow!!! 2007...
Around here, stirring up
the mix of perplexity

And please do correct me
if I'm wrong. You don't understand.
Everything was handed to you Jim Crow.

I worried about meal while
you closed deals.

I worried about bills while
you're look for ways to
kill my people by committing
genocide.

I laid on cold floors with
crackling doors while you're
using our minds as your
intelligence's whore.

Don't get me wrong,
I'm not racist. My family
is made up of bi-racial
faces. And not every
Caucasian is the same.

But for those who are
intolerant. This poems
for you. Jim Crow!
I will continue to be your
threat.

<u>**Volume (noun):**</u>
1. To be highly expressive **or significant**

Acknowledgement

Before I officially end part one of the story I wanted to express my Thanks to those who have made this book possible and guided me through this rough but meaningful terrain called Life.

I want to first acknowledge my God Almighty for creating me with his perfect hands and lavishing the love and gift of Words for he trusted me enough with it to carry out his purpose. There's so many people that I have to thank but I'm going to keep this short and sweet. For those who have been there since the beginning and never left my side(you know who you are) I want to express my gratitude to you and of course the ones that were against me, I too thank you for you were used as my stepping stones. When I decided to compile the poetry into a series of books the message I wanted to promote was empowerment. After all of the experiences and the struggles, I can begin to appreciate each trial for it made me the man that I am today and because of that I am more than willing to open myself up to those who are reading this book. Nonetheless, I especially want to thank <u>YOU</u> for picking up my book and helping my dream to become a reality.

     Thank You!

To be continued….

www.ingramcontent.com/pod-product-compliance
Lightning Source LLC
Chambersburg PA
CBHW020008050426
42450CB00005B/371